ECHOES
OF *Loneliness*

ECHOES
OF *Loneliness*

*Abused and unloved, a little girl listens
for the call of hope.*

By

Diane Troup

ReadersMagnet, LLC

I would like to dedicate this book to my wonderful children, Eric, Christina, Shawn, and Ryan. They have become wonderful young adults, and they are the best accomplishment that I will ever reach. They are more than wonderful children; they are wonderful friends. They have richly blessed my life many times and have made my life even richer with four beautiful and precious granddaughters, Elizabeth, Molly, Allison, and Alexis. May God be with you all and may your paths in life be as beautiful as each of you are.

Table of Contents

Echoes of Silence

I was just a little girl at the age of three
When my whole life came crashing down on me.
I thought that tomorrow the sun would still shine
And no problems would be labeled as only mine.

But the silence echoed in the lonely walls
As I lay and listened to the empty halls.
No parents were there to encourage me to run
Or children to help me have lots of fun.

I craved for someone to smile and say,
"Come outside and join us at play."
But all around me were children older than me
And only adults could I ever see.

Gone were the memories of my brothers I loved so dear
Gone was the laughter I needed to hear.
For my parent thought they had enough
To raise a family seemed just too rough.

So, I cried in my pillow each night
As I shivered alone in such deep fright.
I craved for someone to make me feel whole
As the echoes of silence seeped deep in my soul.

The Treat

The room is so stuffy and hot, and I feel like I can't breathe. My heart is beating so hard, I think it is going to burst open and make a terrible mess. *Where is everyone? Why doesn't Mommy or anyone come to answer my cries of terror? Please, someone help me. I am just a little girl, and I cannot take care of these snakes alone.*

Suddenly, the lights come on and release me from the terror; my heart slows down a little bit. My big brother comes over to sit on my bed. He asks me why I was screaming and crying, but all I can utter is, *"Where is everyone? Where is Mommy?"* Bobby, my big brother of age five, just reaches out to hold a frightened little sister of three and tells me that he doesn't know either.

"Who will help us now that Mommy is gone? He tells me with fear in his little voice too. Together we huddle together as I tell him about my snakes and how I was afraid to move. He smiles and tells me that they were just wrinkles in the rug and holds me until I fall asleep again. Little did I know that as I laid my head down to rest that night, it was a night that was to be the beginning of a different and painful world for me at the tender age of three.

The day was so warm and sunny. The babysitter took my brothers, Bobby, David, Baby Neil, and me to the store for ice-cream. I knew that money was often tight, so when we were taken for a treat, it was a special time indeed. I remember my baby brother being pushed in his little buggy as I skipped merrily with my older brothers. We were in high spirits and full of fun when we arrived home at our house on the hill. As we came in our front door, we were greeted by the back of our mother's head leaving through the back door. I cried because she was leaving without any of us in a big black car. My brothers and I watched as the big black car sped away and out of sight. We never knew that those tears we shed were the beginning of a lifetime of tears we would cry.

Forever my life would be haunted by the picture of a red head full of curls walking away and out of our young lives.

"I am so hungry," I cried to my brother Bob. Although he was only five years old, he was the oldest brother, and now he was in charge of David, age four, me (Diane) age three, and our baby brother who was only a few months old. The baby looked so sick, and we were so hungry, but there were no adults around. Who would help us find something to eat? The cupboards were empty. Bob decided that he needed to get us some food, but where would he get money? He did what need made him do. He walked down to the small store that had provided us with such a happy trip for ice cream just a few days before. This time, though, the storeowner wasn't smiling when Bob took some milk and food for his brothers and sisters. When he questioned Bob, he was horrified to find that there were four small children left in a home with no adult supervision and no food. The authorities were alerted.

Our dad was a businessman with the traveling circus. Whenever there weren't any shows, he would go out on a small boat and gather Spanish moss. Of course, we, as children, didn't know where he was at this time.

We remembered times when we went together on the boat. But at the moment our little minds couldn't tell anyone where he might be.

How horrified and worried he must have been until he could arrange for a ride home to find his children crying and huddled together, yet so alone in the great world. He thought he had left his children at home with his wife. After all, most mothers are very caring for their children, aren't they?

How was a man supposed to raise four children alone and still work and provide for them-especially a man who traveled for a living? Where would we spend the days when he had to be gone, and how would he be able to provide the caring and supervision we needed? He knew he needed help and turned to a friend for some assistance.

"Oh boy, we are going to a new home for a while. We are going to have a real adventure and stay with some friends of Daddy's."

How high my hopes were when I thought about all that was happening. Maybe our bellies wouldn't echo with the empty sounds of hunger. Perhaps we would have a puppy to play with, and we could be a family. Maybe, just maybe I could learn to smile again instead of shedding all those tears that I had been crying.

A New Adventure

A winding hill looked inviting as we drove toward a nice big house.

Is this our new home? Will we be able to run and play in the big yard? Could this mean that my brothers and I are going to see our mother again? Or will this new lady smile and be our mom for a while?

Our hearts were full of expectations, but we were still scared and nervous. Our daddy was there, and he would make sure that everything was okay.

He told us that he would have to leave, but he would return to see us again really soon. There were tears in our eyes as we said goodbye; however, we were so full of adventure that we weren't too worried.

The lady's smile looked so nice, and I like the laughter that I heard rumble from the big man's chest. As sleep claimed that day, my heart felt a little bit better I couldn't wait for the new day so that I could explore our new home. I didn't know when we would see Daddy again, but at the least the dreams and things that scared me so badly wouldn't be able to find us here.

Little did I know, but that that day was one of very few to be repeated. Upon awakening, I found that it was an illusion. Gone was the nice man from the day before. The lady with the smile seemed to have misplaced that too. She seemed almost as afraid as we children in the days to come. She would try to hug and calm our fears, but she was just as helpless and afraid to do anything to help herself, let alone four small children.

"Stop! Please stop hitting my brother!" I cried. As soon as I spoke the words, I was next to feel the bit of the nasty old belt. I hated the smell of beer on the man's breath and hated to hear hateful fighting all the time. My daddy never spoke to us with that awful voice. I couldn't understand why he was so mean, but what scared me so much was that the man liked to clean his guns. His wife would try to hug us and tell us things would get better, but even she was afraid when the yelling started, and we smelled an awful smell on his breath. I couldn't wait until Daddy came back to visit-he would know what to do. I am not sure how many days or weeks went by; it just seemed like such a long time to me. Every day without my daddy or mommy seemed to be such a long time.

Finally, after what seemed like forever, Daddy came to visit us, and we were so excited. Things would be all better. He would take us all back home, and we would be happy and wouldn't need to worry. But when I saw Daddy there were tears in his eyes; I don't know why I had such a funny feeling in the pit of my tummy. Daddy took us children out to have some quiet time and said that he needed to make some changes. Uncle Brad was too angry, and he had a problem with his temper. Aunt Dorothy was worried about him hitting and hurting us or worse yet, using one of his guns when he was drinking that funny-smelling stuff that my daddy called beer. I did not understand the big word that he used, but he told us we were going to go to an orphanage. I just knew that he was going to take us somewhere while he had to go away again.

I wonder, *what is this place? Will there be someone there with a big belt, or will we be safe and happy?*

Daddy tried to assure us, but how could he when his eyes were full of tears that made awful tracks down his cheeks? I was so frightened, but all little girls trust their daddy. He was so big and strong and would always protect me.

Daddy took us to a big place with several children running around. It had a nice swing set; maybe it wouldn't be so bad. As Daddy talked to some people, a lady came and led me away by my hand. I looked back and said I wanted to stay with my brothers, but she told me to come with her. She seemed so tall, and I was so afraid, but Daddy smiled and told me to be a good girl and listen to the nice lady. With tears I followed the lady away from my brothers, away from Daddy, and away from the family that was so dear to me. Little did I know that I was walking toward a lifetime of heartbreak and tears.

The Orphanage

So, this is an orphanage, I thought. *There were so many beds in one room. Does this mean that I will have that many sisters and brothers with me now? Can I play with them, or should perhaps my "sisters" can read me stories? Where are my brothers and why can't I see them?*

Where are my brothers? Why can't I see them? I feel so alone and afraid. There are so many beds and a big box of toys, perhaps they will come later. I hoped so. I did not like the quiet too much, and the shadows seemed to make me feel like there was danger coming after me. It was hard to breathe when there were so many shadows.

A little later I heard a lot of noise and some girls giggling. Soon the room was full of several girls who all just stopped and stared at me. They were all older and just getting home from school. One girl stepped forward and told me her name was Debbie. She introduced me to another girl a bit older than me and her name was Linda. The other names and faces blurred in my mind as I searched frantically for my brothers. I don't know how I would have made it through the first days if Debbie had not held me and let me cry on her shoulder. I was so lonely and afraid. Every morning they would all dress and leave me alone to face the shadows and quiet as they went to school.

I would try to make sense of the things that Debbie and Linda told me. They explained that an orphanage was a fancy name for a place for kids who have no one to love them. I couldn't understand why I was there. I had a Daddy who loved me He told me he loved me, so why was I here? There must have been some mistake. When I told Debbie that, she would say, "No, they are looking for new Mommies and Daddies for us all." I was so confused; tears were my constant companion as I waited each day for school to end.

The day was warm and sunny. I was eager to go outside and play on the playground. It was lonely there, as I was the only little girl in the orphanage who did not go to school. Sunday school and church would have been a different change, but I had no nice clothing so I could not go. I looked longingly out to the swings and hoped someone would come and take me outside. How happy I was when I heard someone say, "What a wonderful day, Diane, would you like to go outside and play?"

I ran to the swing set and crawled up on the swing. I wanted to fly so high that I could fly away from the pain and confusion. *Why had life taken such a hard fall? What* had *I done? Where were the people I loved? How much pain could one little heart hold?*

But there in the distance, just beyond the fence, I spied such a welcome sight My knees shook as I ran toward the fence. I cried for all my little voice was worth for there in the distance were the two of the most precious people in my heart at that time. My big brothers were on the swings in the distance, playing with some other boys. Finally, I could play with my brothers.

Perhaps they would give me a big hug, we could figure out what went so wrong and why such a terrible mistake was made. Maybe they knew where Daddy was and could tell someone that we didn't belong in an orphanage.

My big brother Bob, saw me waving and heard me crying out for him. He and "Goliath" both ran over to the fence to say hello. Some lady came and stood over us, and she didn't look very happy. I just wanted to talk to my brothers. I wanted them to come and push me on the swing the way they used to. Why couldn't they come over and play? Why did they have to stay on the other side of the fence?

"This is the playground for the boys, and you have your playground for the girls", I was told. We were permitted to speak to each other for a few minutes, but soon were ushered back inside. The shadows were all that were left to be with me again.

I don't remember walking inside; I don't remember much of anything that day, except the pain. I wanted my big brothers. Where was our baby brother? Why were we here? Was there something really bad that I did to make this happen? So many questions with so few answers were exhausting for someone so small. My world was scary, and I was frightened.

"Please, please, someone help me," I cried, for my tears were heavy and I was alone. I truly knew what the world "orphanage" meant, and I did not like it one bit.

My Christmas Wish

I can see the sun shining in the sky so bright
But I feel like I am living in a perpetual night.
I turn my face upward searching for the warmth of
the sun there
Wishing for someone to show me they care.

The skies are painted a pretty blue,
But my world is covered with a heavy dew.
I see the clouds all fluffy and white in the air
But they seem like cotton bundles that hold all my care.

Why can't I see through this awful rain?
Why must I stumble around in such pain?
I am only a little child, you see,
But life has no color, no promise for me.

All I really want for Christmas this year
Is healing from all the pain and the fear.
I don't want new toys, for I've forgotten how to smile
I don't want new shoes, for I'm too tired to walk the
extra mile.

Please, someone, take pity and help to find
A healing presence for my heart and my mind.
For all I want for Christmas are parents of my own
to love
So, I can see all the beauty from God above.

A New Day

"Wake up, sleepy head," I heard someone say. The voice sounded friendly, but my heart hurt too much to appreciate it. I knew the ladies at the orphanage wanted to make me smile, but what for? Was there anything left to smile about?

Debbie ran over and told me it was Saturday. She said there was a big surprise waiting for me: I had a visitor. I just knew that my Daddy was coming to take us home and would fix the mistake that was made. I told Debbie, "You see, I do have someone that loves me." She smiled and patted my hand. She was so much older, but I would make her see.

I looked down the stairs and knew that my face must have reflected the sunshine that day, for there standing below was the answer to all my pain. My Daddy stood there with a smile on his face, his arms reaching out to me. I couldn't run down those stairs fast enough. When I jumped into his arms, I felt like I was home again. My Daddy was my hero, and he would make everything better. I just knew it. Not only was he here to hold me, but he had brought presents. I did not understand why my brothers weren't there too, but I guess I was the first one he picked up. Maybe it meant that I was his favorite or something. I felt so proud, and suddenly I remembered how to smile.

Daddy gave me a big doll. It had a beautiful dress and some shoes. I was amazed at her pretty painted face, and I hugged her to me. He produced another package that was colorfully wrapped. It was a slate with some chalk and a coloring book. I told him I would treasure them forever and would take really good care of the presents when we went home, because at the orphanage I didn't have anything of my own. Everything was going to be okay. I was going home with my Daddy, my hero, who could fix anything.

Something was funny about my Daddy's face. He stopped smiling and hugged me so close it hurt. I patted his face and told him it was okay because we were going home. We could pick up the boys and the baby and go back home. Maybe Mommy would be there, but if not, who cared? My Daddy would be there, and he was all I needed. I could hardly wait for him to tell me all the good news.

Instead, he got down on his knee and told me a story about a man who could not take care of his small children and still work. He said he loved me and his sons, but he wanted something more for them. What could be more important than being together? I did not understand. He explained that he was going to have to go away and would not be back for a very long time. He said he was going to sign papers so that the people at the orphanage could look for another Mommy or Daddy for me. I was to be a good girl and not cry. Someday I would understand. I remember a big hug and kiss and a lot of tears. I remember someone coming and leading me back upstairs, and the last memory I have of my Daddy was watching him sink to the floor, crying like a broken man. I didn't understand what it all meant.

The only thing I did know was that I was as afraid as I had never been afraid. Was Debbie, right? Would I always live in this place called an orphanage, a place where there were no Mommies or Daddies?

Tears, tears, and more tears soaked my pillow as I lay there. I didn't know if it was day or night. What did it matter? I was alone. Daddy explained to me that the boys weren't allowed to come to the girls' side and that our baby was in the hospital at the orphanage. I was so sure, so sure he was going to fix things. He was my Daddy. But all he did that day was kill my spirit. I was no longer a little girl. I was a shell of a person; I no longer cared what happened around me. One day would fade into another. I was just one of the shadows.

Tears

Tears upon my pillow, trying to hide
The truth that I am crying so desperately inside
Tears upon my pillow, sobs so late at night,
Signs that life just doesn't seem to be working out quite
right.

A tiny drop of water seems like no weight at all,
But then you're the one who's crying, they really don't
seem small.
Drops of tiny misery that roll down my face
As I try so desperately in life to find my place.
But the tears are but a tiny thing that seems to try and say
"Please help me as I stumble and try to find my way."
Be patient with this little child as my tears fall down like
rain,
For I am trying oh so hard to make sense of all this pain.

My New Day

The sun was shining outside as someone bounced on my bed. Debbie showed me her bright smile. I never knew how he could still smile when we were all alone. She tried so hard to make me smile, and I guess sometimes she succeeded. After all, she was the closest thing to family I had. That day she had a small package for me. She told me that the lady at the desk had told her to give it to me. She was excited, but I didn't know why. She told me to hurry up and open it, and I would have a new sweater. When I asked her how she knew, she replied, "Everyone gets a new sweater when they are going to meet a new Mom or Dad."

"Oh, I thought, those illusive things, a mom and Dad. But I had a glimmer of hope; perhaps she was right.

As I tore open the package, I found a small yellow sweater. It was so soft and had tiny buttons down the front. It had been so long since I had anything new, and this was very pretty. Could it really mean that I was going to meet a new Mom and Dad? Maybe I wasn't the bad girl I thought I had been. Maybe someone would want me. My heart was troubled, and I was afraid, but like the strength of the youth, I found a spark of hope and excitement.

Soon, as I was told, a big station wagon came up to the door. Inside were my two big brothers, and to my great surprise, my baby brother. It seemed like a dream to me. We were all going to get a new Mommy and Daddy. It was the day that Debbie talked about. Maybe she was right. I would be sad not to see her, but I saw my brothers and we were too excited to worry about anything else. It is funny how a smile can reappear when you think you forgot how to use it.

I could barely contain my excitement as I was ushered to the hallway. I felt like a princess with my

pretty yellow sweater My little heart was beating so fast
that I was afraid it might fly away.

I could barely keep myself from running out toward
the big station wagon sitting outside the door, I paused
a minute to turn and wave goodbye to my two tearful
friends. Debbie and Linda stood and waved and gave
trembling smiles. Their smiles touched my heart, and
I knew that I would miss them, but it strengthened
my resolve that I would get what they told me I never
would, a new Mommy and Daddy.

My excitement turned to genuine joy as I saw my big
brothers sitting inside that car. It seemed like forever
since I had last seen them or had been close enough to
get a hug. To add to my feeling of wonder, I spied a lady
sitting in the front seat, holding a tiny bundle. When I
peered into the blankets, my eyes filled with tears and
my heart flipped right over in my chest. There, nestled
in those blankets, was my own very dear baby brother.
How long had it been since I had seen his tiny face or
heard his little coos?

Wow! Could today be any better? I felt like I was
riding on top of the world. When I had woken up in
my bed with all the other beds in a row, little had I

known that this day would hold so many surprises. Not only did I get a brand-new sweater and got to see my brothers, but we were all going to meet our new Mommy and Daddy. I could barely keep from smiling, even though every once in a while, a question would enter my mind.

Would our new Mommy and Daddy treat us like our other Daddy did, or would he have a big belt to use on us? These thoughts were fleeting; however, with the innocence and resilience of a child, I knew that our new home would be a new fun adventure for us all. I loved talking and teasing with my brothers as the countryside rushed by.

Gone were the big, tall buildings where we grew up and now there were many barns and big houses. Was our new home going to be in the new, pretty countryside? Would we soon leave all the hustle and bustle and noise behind us and finally find some peace?

Soon the car turned into a pretty yard with a big barn and a great big house. There was a big tree that hung low and offered what looked to be an inviting place to play. Everywhere I looked there was space.

How much fun my new family and I could share exploring this place.

"Look, boys, here comes a lady and a man. I bet this is our new Mommy and Daddy." I said with excitement mixed with a bit of fear and shyness. It was really exciting to meet the lovely lady and the tall man with the big smile, the lady offered her hand as I scrambled out of the car. We walked toward the house, and she talked softly to me as she held my hand. I was in wonder at her soft voice and warm smile.

But wait, why didn't my brothers get out of the car? And the lady who held my baby brother, she got back into the car with him too. Why didn't they come and meet the nice lady and man? They were to be their new Mommy and Daddy, too, weren't they?

A scream built from my toes to the very middle of my heart. The car was moving away rather quickly, and my precious brothers were still inside. I wanted to scream in frustration and pain, but I couldn't even find the strength to whimper anymore.

Please, oh please, my little heart cried, *I just got to see my brothers after such a long time. Don't take them away again. Please, I need my brothers. I have no one else left"*.

I was too young to comprehend it all, and suddenly I was too tired to even try.

There must have been some mistake. The day had started out so special. My heart felt so full of happiness, and now it hurt so badly I could barely stand it.

As I cried and watched that big car drive away, I spied my two brothers looking out the window, waving frantically. Once again, my old companion had snuck up on me and my eyes were filled with those familiar tears, and I could barely see. I gazed in shock as David and "Goliath" waved frantically, and I noticed that they had the same companion as me, tears! *How much pain can one little girl bear? How can they do this to me?? What kind of monster am I that everyone I love is being torn away from me? It must be my fault.* Those tears would forever be in my mind, leaving scars and echoes of loneliness in my heart.

I don't know if I can survive this pain anymore. Do I even want to try? The pain is so great. All I want to do is cry until I can cry no more. I don't want to eat, I don't want to play, and I don't even want the new clothes or toys offered to me. I just want the pain to go away. Can a little girl die of a broken heart?

I surely hoped so because the pain was so deep and hurt every part of my body, my heart and, and my mind. I knew I should've been happy about getting a new home, but I didn't know how to be happy. I didn't think I would ever be happy again. I cried myself to sleep each night, and with the morning light a new batch was waiting to torment me.

A few days later, the nice lady who was going to be my Mommy said she had a surprise for me. "I know that you have been very sad, and your little heart is hurting because you miss your brothers, and we are going to find out if we can keep in touch with your big brothers. I have an even bigger surprise for you. We are going to bring your baby brother to live here too. We want to adopt both you and your brother."

At that time, I did not know what "adopt" meant, but she patiently told me that it meant that they had picked out both my brother and me to be their children, and together we would be a brand-new family.

Perhaps the tears weren't quite as heavy that night as I thought about seeing my baby brother. I didn't even mind when they told me that they would change both his name and mine. I liked the name Ty for my brother and my name would be Diane which I liked better than Lucille. Maybe there was some hope after all. Perhaps I would be able to be a little happy. Maybe with my brother at my house I would be able to smile and feel like a little girl again. As I curled up to go to sleep, I promised myself that I would try to stop crying all the time and make my new parents love me. Perhaps then they would not turn their backs and walk away from us like our other parents did.

Big Cars

How I hate great big cars
For they are a symbol of many scars.
A big car carried my Mommy away.
And a big car ate up my brothers one day.

I used to wish we could own a car.
And get inside and drive really far.
But alas my Mommy found a big car one day
A big black car carried her forever away.

In the orphanage I carried a little hope.
After all, it helped me to cope.
I dreamed of another Mommy and Dad
Who might help me not to be so sad?

This Mommy and Daddy would own their own car
And together we would all go far.
We would laugh and we would sing
What joys I thought it all would bring.

One day a big car stopped at the orphanage gate.
I was so excited; I could hardly wait.
Inside were my brothers I dearly missed so much
And a kind lady with a gentle touch.

But what is happening? What can I do?
The big car stopped and let me off without you!
My brothers disappeared in the night
And I have been left with no spirit or fight.

I never want to own a car so big, you see
For it is a reminder of the scars dealt to me.
The big cars that I have seen aren't so nice,
For they brought me a big painful price.

Soiled Goods

"Now be a good girl, Diane, and maybe, just maybe they will tell you where your brothers are."

How hard I strove to be a good little girl. It wasn't easy to be totally quiet when I knew there was a man called a judge who was going to make a decision that would mean that I would have a new Mommy and Daddy. I wanted so badly to be adopted. I wanted to know that I had someone who would love me and make my baby brother and me a part of their family. More than anything else, I wanted to know where my big brothers were taken. I miss them so badly, and I wanted to know they were going to be with me again. I tried so hard to sit quietly and do as I was told while my parents were inside talking to the judge about the whole adoption thing. I didn't understand what adoption really meant; I just knew that perhaps I would get a new Mommy and Daddy and find out where my big brothers were.

What did I do? I tried so hard to be good. Why can't I know where my big brothers are now? I cried so hard and begged to know why I couldn't see my big brothers. I wanted my big brothers; after all, they were my anchors when my other "Mommy" went away. Mommy tried to explain to me that the other people who were going to adopt my big brothers did not want us to see each other. There was nothing that they could do.

After the court proceedings, a brokenhearted little girl followed her new parents and baby brother back to their new home. My name was changed, and I was a new little girl, yet I carried the same painful lonely heart. Perhaps this Mommy and Daddy will take away some of that pain. Sometimes the pain was so bad that it was hard to sleep at night, especially that night when another disappointment was given to me.

Late that night I cried myself to sleep. *Could it be that they knew my terrible secret? Did someone tell them what a bad little girl I really am? Will a big car come and take me to another home tomorrow?* Terrible thoughts followed me into the darkness until I was too weary to keep my eyes open. I never told the awful thing that happened to me, yet someway, somehow, they must have found out. I lay there quietly and thought back to that terrible day not long ago.

Just a few days before the adoption I was so happy thinking that I would be getting my new Mommy and Daddy after all. After all, they cared enough to get my baby brother when my heart hurt so much. They sure were special people. I worked on the farm, packing eggs into crates. I felt like a big girl because I was able to help with the chores.

Suddenly the door opened, and the young man who worked on the farm came inside. He was a young man in high school, and he often helped with the farm work. I knew him from being there before, and he would often joke with me and tell me I was a cute little girl. At first it didn't seem so bad when he gave me a hug. But then it didn't feel right when he started touching me places where I had never been touched before. I told him to stop, that I did not like it. I was just a tiny child and did not have the strength or the knowledge to fight off his advances. He pushed me onto the table where we packed the eggs and did things to me that were hurtful and embarrassing. Now I was a dirty, bad little girl. No one would ever love me if they knew what I had done. I was so afraid and hurt so badly. What could I do? I promised not to tell and locked away that painful day in my little mind and terrified heart forever. I never wanted to risk not getting a family that I so desperately wanted.

But is it possible? Could it be? Did someone tell them what happened and is that why I cannot know where my brothers are? Was I a bad little girl that no one could ever learn to love? What will happen to me? Where am I going to go? Fear haunted me in every waking moment, and I carried shame and pain like a heavy cloak that I was made to wear. How much pain can one little child carry on such a frail back? I didn't know then, but I would learn to bear all of it and so much more.

Would I ever know a peaceful night of sleep? I was so tired and frightened, but when I closed my eyes at night, I dreamed that same awful dream. I would fade back to the day when my real Mommy walked away from us. We would come in the back door and there she was, walking out the front door. Only this time it was different. It wasn't the back of her head that I saw, but rather my new parents walking away from me. The dream would haunt me for a long time, reoccurring so often that it was almost an extension or direct relative of my other haunting companion, tears. I feared the shadows, for it seemed they were hiding my secrets, yet I feared the sunlight, for perhaps it would shine some light on who and what I really was. I was soiled, someone who was so unlovable that the only constants in my life were the tears, pain, and the Echoes of loneliness.

Our New Baby

A few years had gone by since I had decided to try and make the best of things in my new life. There were still some nights that the tears would visit me, but those nights were growing less and less. I felt like I had a second chance at being a family, and I sure did love my little brother. Believe me, we still fought, and sometimes hit each other, but mostly I was so thankful for his presence that he could do no wrong.

Day by day I was beginning to feel more like a normal little girl and the pain seemed to be more of a shadow that would come out only occasionally.

I loved to run in the fields and to wade in the cool, clean water. It was so different to have a home to live in and not to be living in the back of a huge truck. I could close my eyes and remember when my brothers and I would travel with our patents to the various circus stops. I could still remember the songs they sang as "Mommy" would come out to dance. I would sometimes sing those songs when I was playing, but my new Mommy and Daddy would scold me and sometime slap me, saying they were not nice. I didn't understand why, but I wanted to make them like me so I would try to listen. My heart felt so much better when I was out in the sunshine, and I could run and play.

One day was an especially happy day because Mommy told me some news that made me so happy that I could barely contain my excitement. "Today we will go and get you a new baby brother." She said.

I kept dancing and singing and hoping the time would come soon. I barely knew how to stand still, and the drive to the hospital to pick up my brand-new baby brother seemed to take so long. I would sometimes talk to Jesus and tell him how much I missed my brothers; I secretly thought that maybe he was sending this baby brother to replace the ones I had lost.

I don't remember seeing a more beautiful sight than that day when my mother came out with a tiny bundle wrapped up in a little blanket. My mommy explained that we would call him Robbie Douglas. What a beautiful name. and what a beautiful brother. I was so happy. The sun shone a little brighter, for I had two brothers again. Ty was only 3 years old, and I was six. It seemed like there was a way to push away the pain and not let it make me sad so much. I don't know why some lady did not want that beautiful baby boy, but I was so thankful that my Mommy and Daddy did. I was slowly learning that adoption meant that we were a family, even though different people had given birth to us.

What a nice thought. To share babies is so nice, I thought

I was a big sister who could not hold my brother or hug him enough. Hugs weren't really an everyday occurrence in our household, but I couldn't help myself. I love his pretty blue eyes and his blond hair. He must have been the most beautiful little brother in the whole world.

Together we grew and learned about many new things. My brother, Ty, and I were close, but with the new baby now, I was even happier. I wanted to learn to do more things and make my parents smile. It seemed hard to please them some days, but I was sure going to try.

I was a big sister, and I knew I had to act like one. No one would ever hurt the little baby boy like my brothers, and I were hurt. I knew I was only a little girl, but I felt the protective possessiveness of an adult's heart. The little boy was just one more way to heal the many scars left on my heart.

A Second Chance

A baby born by some young lass,

Was she someone of the working class?

Or was she just a young child too

Who gave birth to this baby with eyes of blue?

I marvel at this baby, so perfect and dear.

I want to always hug him and hold him near.

I pray for Jesus to protect him with his love

For he is a great blessing from God above.

This little baby will never quite know

How his own birth would help me to grow,

He doesn't know the scars that I hide

For I am not always crying on the outside.

Precious brother, I love you much.

May you always be handled with a loving touch.

For you mean so very much, you see

For you are a second chance for me.

A change to regain what was taken one day

When my other brothers were taken away.

Someday when we are bigger, I hope you will see

You are healer of the heart for me.

What A Surprise

School could sometimes be a pain, but I was proud that fifth grade seemed to be so easy. I brought home good grades most of the time, and the teacher seemed to like me. One morning he began calling out names, telling us to line up in the order our names were called. He told us that this was about a test that we had taken the week before. I was getting kind of nervous because he didn't call my name, and there weren't many who were left standing in line. *Oh no*, I thought, *I must have done really poorly, but the others sitting down are kids who seem to be doing okay in school too.* Finally, I was the only one left sitting in my seat. I was afraid of what he was going to say. I know sometimes my mind wandered during class, but I thought I was doing so well. It was my last year in elementary school, and I was trying hard. My parents would be so angry at me, I shook as the teacher finally called my name.

With trembling legs and my head held low, I stumbled up to stand in line. I was so ashamed that tears were ready to fall.

"Now, our teacher said, look at who is standing next to you. I have something I want to tell you. Diane, you were called last because you had the highest grade, and you really number one in the standings."

With deep relief I smiled. My smile was so bright I could have saved some electricity that day. I was proud that I had finally done something right. Perhaps now my parents would smile and tell me I had done a good job.

The class gave me some self-confidence and helped me to achieve some milestones in my education. I finally felt like life was a bit brighter for me.

I even felt like friends were going to be an important part of my life; however, at recess one of my friends came up to me. She was talking about my mother. "Your mother is pregnant", she said. I was in the fifth grade, and maybe I was getting smarter, but I did not know what that meant. I was very naïve, as this was not something that we talked about. The girls laughed at me when I didn't know what they were talking about.

I had noticed that my mom was getting bigger, but I didn't really think too much of it. I listened as the girls explained that my mom was going to have a baby. I was hurt that I didn't know but was really proud when I thought about it. Now another one of my brothers would be replaced. How could I have thought that I am not sure, but it was like a big band-aid was being put on a sore spot in my heart.

With joy I waited until I got home that day. I told Mom what the girls had told me, and she said, "Yes, sometime before Christmas I will have a new baby brother or sister." Of course, I wanted a boy, another brother for sure. When the time came for the baby to be born, I was so excited. I cherished that little bundle. His name was to be David. What a wonderful name, as it was the same name as my brother who was taken from my young life. I knew I would love him as much as I did my other brother, David. I thought it was the most beautiful name in the world and he was the most beautiful baby on this earth.

I loved being a big sister, and I carried him around so much that when he got old enough to walk, he would often cry for me to carry him. He was such a sweet little boy, and he would never know how much his birth meant to me. At night I could go to sleep with visions of Ty, Robbie, and David all playing with me. I felt that perhaps I would be able to smile and forget all about the other life I had known. Little did I know that puberty was nearing, and I would be mixed up and full of hate.

Crying Uncle

Sometimes I didn't know why all I wanted to do was cry. One day I would feel like a little girl, but then the next I would realize that my body was changing, and I was not ready. I didn't want to grow up; I missed too much time being a child. But life has its way of making us all grow up.

There was so much to do on a farm. Some days I really hated that there didn't seem to be a spare minute, while other times I really cherished the time I spent packing the eggs. I tried to sort out some of those confusing emotions that seemed to follow me. One day I felt like I was still a lonely little girl, then the next minute I felt like I was becoming a woman. Strange feelings that I did not always understand would come over me and confuse me. The quiet and peacefulness of repeating the chores seemed to calm me and help me to feel more at peace.

I heard someone outside the egg room door. At first it didn't bother me, but then I started to think about how many times my uncle had been surprising me when I was alone working. He had begun asking me more and more about boys and how they made me feel. He always told me that I was growing up into a pretty young lady. No one else ever told me that, and it did make me feel good. But for some reason it also made me feel nervous. I was not really sure why, but so many times I would find him watching me, and a funny feeling would come over me. I felt like something was wrong, but I couldn't really understand what or why. He began giving me hugs when he left if we were alone. He had never done that before, and he would never do it in front of anyone. I couldn't help but get a bit scared when he found me alone. The egg room was usually a place where I liked to reflect on things and find comfort in the repetition of working with the eggs.

Occasionally, though, I would get a funny feeling, like the place held a bad memory for me, but I couldn't remember why. (Years later I remembered that the egg room was where I had experienced a traumatic incident that colored my mind forever).

I hoped it was one of the foster boys or my brothers coming to help me. I wouldn't mind too much if someone disturbed my quiet time if I could joke and tease with them for a while. Sometimes I felt so lucky to have been given another chance, and I was so thankful that I had brothers who weren't going to be taken away from me.

The door opened and it was my uncle who came in, smiling. "I see your mom and Dad went somewhere. Are you working here all alone?"

I wondered why he would ask me that, he knows that I do this chore. He knows when it is time to pack eggs and he knows that I am always here at this time of the day. Oh well, I am not going to worry. He is smiling and joking and seems to be in a wonderful mood, I thought to myself.

He brought some candy and gum and offered me some as he talked about different things and made me laugh.

All of a sudden, he approached me and pulled the basket from my hands. When I was startled, he told me that he wanted to help me with the heavy baskets. He said they were heavier than a young lady should lift. He sounded so concerned, and he seemed to understand me more than any other adult ever had. He encouraged me to talk about how I would sometimes get sad, and he told me that he would always listen.

As he sat the basket on the table, he reached out and pulled me close to him. "I just want a hug," he said, but he was holding me too tightly. The nervous feelings started to scare me, and I tried to pull away. He whispered kind words about caring for me and how he wished he could have adopted me. He told me that he wanted to show me how much he really cared for me. Although I craved to have someone love me, I knew this wasn't right.

As you become a young lady, you will begin to feel special emotions. Your parents may tell you they are wrong to feel, or you might learn that they can be dangerous things to feel, but don't believe it. When we start to feel these things, it is normal, it means you are growing up. It means you will be able to love more deeply, and the feelings lead to bigger and better feelings," he said.

Suddenly his hands were all over me, and he was touching me in places I knew were wrong. I felt funny in my tummy, and it was not all together unpleasant, but I knew it was wrong. I became more and more afraid because he didn't seem to hear me when I asked him to stop. His lips were on mine, and he told me that he was just showing me how much he really loved me. The funny feelings were gone; I was truly afraid and started to cry. He would not let me go, and I was now shaking with fear. He was so much bigger and stronger than I was, and I was afraid to talk back to an adult. My parents taught me that to talk back means more pain, and I was so tired of being hit.

What do I do? I am afraid. His hands are hurting me. This pain is harsh and so humiliating. My mother taught me that my body is private, and he is invading so many private parts of me. I am so afraid. He is breathing really fast; he looks like he cannot hear me beg him to stop, I thought to myself.

Suddenly there was a noise outside. "Hey Diane…" I had never been so thankful. "I'm almost finished…" I said. Thankfully, my uncle seemed to hear it and stopped touching me. He knew that at any minute my brother could walk in the door. He looked down at me and saw the tears and told me not to say anything. No one would understand. He told me again that he loved me and that someday soon he would show me how much.

I didn't know what to say, and I was afraid, so I didn't say anything. After all, what does a thirteen-year-old know about such things?

I kept thinking; I hope I am not alone with him anytime soon. Maybe he will forget about what he did and told me.

The days seemed to follow one after another, and my uncle would now often stop by to visit. He came to help with bailing hay and other chores. He came often without my aunt. She was such a sweet person, and I really liked her. I didn't feel nervous when she was with my uncle.

More and more I was interrupted when I was packing eggs by my uncle. There were times when he would come into the barn when I was doing chores. He seemed to find more and more time to tell me how deeply he cared for me. His hands were always reaching to touch me, and he was trying more and more often to kiss me. How could I make him understand that he was scaring me and that I wanted him to stop? He didn't seem to listen to what I said. He became bolder and more insistent of showing me things that he said all young women should know. I knew that was all wrong and I begged him to stop, but he surprised me many times.

I knew I needed to find a way to stop it happening. I didn't know exactly how, but I did know I was becoming more and more afraid. I knew I needed to talk to someone, so I was pleased when I was told to help Mother with some chores and no one else was in the house. I wanted so much to talk to someone, and I just hoped she would listen to me.

"Mom, I have a problem. My Uncle just will not leave me alone. He does things that me so afraid, and I know they are wrong." After answering many questions, she told me that she would talk to my dad. I hoped she could make things right I knew he wouldn't understand.

Of course, I was right. Dad did not understand, Mom did not understand. No one could understand how afraid I was. I was told that I probably wanted him to do these things to me.

After all, I was from "bad blood" as I had been told before. My birth parents were never really good, and I had probably inherited some of their terrible habits. I was told I was "trash" and would never amount to anything in life. I was told I probably encouraged him. They even said that they thought something was going on with the two of us, but they thought I wanted it to happen. Once again, I realized I was not worthy of anyone's love. I was not able to make them understand that I had told them because I wanted it to stop. I wanted the pain and humiliation to stop. But alas, the humiliation was just starting. I was questioned, poked fun at, and told I was just a waste of space on this earth.

Will life ever get any easier for me? Will I always be alone? I just want someone to understand me. I want someone to care, even just a little. My mind is so burdened, and my heart is so heavy. Perhaps what they say is right. Perhaps I should spare everyone and just make myself disappear. After all, there isn't anyone who would really miss me. We get rid of the trash on a regular basis, so maybe I should just do everyone a favor and take the trash out of this world myself, I thought.

Not A Game Anymore

The bus ride home was long, and sometimes I got to talking to my friend a bit. She did not really understand all that I was going through. After all, she was the apple of her mom's and dad's eye. She seemed so happy, and she always showed me something new that she got or something special her family did together. I called her a friend, but I often wondered what she would say if she knew how much I envied her. What would she think if she would have known that sometimes I got so jealous of her that I wanted to hit her? She was so lucky, but she complained about how she wanted to go here or do this, and her parents wouldn't let her. I just wished I had someone who cared enough to say no out of concern and not out of trying to hurt me a little bit more. Some days I wanted to tell her just how lucky she really was.

Maybe today is that day, I thought to myself. After all, perhaps she should not always be so happy. So, what if she knows that I am hurting, and she feels a little bad? So, what if she hears that not everyone is lucky as she is?

I felt so full of hurt that I didn't know what to do. I knew it was wrong but sometimes I wished I could make someone feel some of the pain so I wouldn't feel so all alone. I would have liked to see the look on her face if she had known that the whole time, I was listening to her, I was thinking of how much I hated her for her happiness. Life was so confusing, and I didn't like feeling that way, but I was too hurt to care anymore. I just wanted to tell her that the person sitting beside her was nothing but a waste of time and space. I wouldn't though, because I was always afraid that maybe she would have agreed with them. I didn't trust anyone anymore, so why would someone who was my age be any different than from all the others in my life? So, I sat quietly and listened to someone else's happiness.

Finally, when she stopped talking, I said, "I feel really bad. I was thinking about taking a trip down to the creek to check out the bridge from the top. I wonder how it would feel to swim with the fishes. She said that it makes me feel nervous." I laughed and made it sound like a game. "Don't worry, I said, it is just a thought that flashed through my mind."

Little did she or anyone else know that those thoughts had been haunting my waking moments, tormenting me at night. It seemed like an answer to stop all the hurting.

"Just a game, I said, to see what you would say." She laughed too, and we talked about some insignificant thing until we reached our homes.

The weekend came with bright sunshine. The sun lit the day in the sky, but not in my heart. I felt so cold and alone. Every Sunday I liked to walk down to the creek and watch the water float by. It seemed to quiet some of the demons that followed me through most of my days. I listened to the birds sing and stared at the light glittering off the water. The beauty usually was able to calm me, but this day I felt as restless as a kite on a windy day.

My mind was racing, and the water seemed to be calling my name. *Just a quick look, just to see how high it really might be to fall. Just a game… how bit a splash I might make. A game to see how the wind would feel on my face as I stand there, overlooking the water.*

"Just a game," I repeated to myself as I climbed up on the bridge's rails. Standing there, the wind caressed my face. No one had ever caressed my face in this crazy mixed-up world.

The wind, the bird's songs, the sunshine on the water, it was all mesmerizing. I wanted to be a part of that peace. Perhaps if I just took one tiny step forward the pain would be gone.

"Just a game, "I reminded myself. "Yes, a game to make them all sorry that they never cared. A game where the winner gets to find the body of a worthless little girl who no one could ever love." Yes, it was just a game, a game that I was now ready to play. After all, I was still a child. I was sure that God would understand and forgive me. I didn't want to think anymore. It is time to play the game. I would be the winner in this game, because the hurting would finally stop.

Just as I was ready to take the final step that would end the game, I heard someone calling my name,

Why, oh why, did one of my brothers have to come down here today? I come here alone all the time, and no one ever looks for me, I thought.

But wait, it is my little brother. I cannot do this with him around. I cannot let him see this. He is smaller than I am. Why would one person who means so much to me, the replacement for the other brothers that were taken from me, why would he come around at this very moment? Well, I guess the game is over and the world will have to put up with this worthless person a bit longer.

The Special Medicine

Oh, how lonely some days could be. School was for learning, but sometimes the lessons I learned there I could do without. There was a girl who liked to call me names and make me feel as worthless as I was told I was. Would I ever find peace? To be honest, it wasn't as if many children talked to me like that. I did have friends and the neighborhood boys treated me nicely. They would even stand up for me if someone got rude. But this one girl, she was so mean, and I don't know why I let it bother me so much. Someday she will get hers, I thought, but really some days I just think she is another person who knows the truth.

How I longed to have someone truly care for me, someone to look at me and smile and mean it. Someone to put their arms around me and tell me nice things and not want something in return that I knew wasn't right. I just wanted to feel like someone worthwhile.

Will this ever happen to me? Or will I always be the girl who walks through the hallways of school looking down at the floor, hoping no one really sees the pain I carry like a cloak?

It seemed like any other day. Little did I know that this day would change my world yet again. Little did I know that this day would give me hope and teach me how to smile and mean it.

As I walked down the hallway, I heard someone whistle, but I paid no mind, as that was not something someone would do for me. How wrong I was! Someone lightly touched my arm and said, "What's so interesting on the floor?" As I looked up, I met the most beautiful blue eyes I have ever seen. Standing there was someone I had known for a while but never very well. There was a brief time in church when his older brother had flirted with me. He came to see me, but my parents put an end to that. They did not encourage any friendships for me, especially not with boys. This had been a low point in my life, so I never grieved for a friendship that had never bloomed.

Standing there was his brother, and I realized that he was a really cute guy. Why had I never seen it before? I was surprised as he walked beside me and asked me to meet him at my locker after school.

As I walked away, my heart felt a bit lighter. Bobby was a really nice guy, and he actually took time to talk to me.

But could this be a cruel game or a joke? After all, why would someone like him want to spend time with me? He isn't the most popular person in school, but he was always nice to me at church and Bible School.

I was still very happy to have someone walk down the hallway beside me that morning. Suddenly the day looked quite promising. As I neared my locker, I must have been smiling a bit. The girl at the locker next to me was a friend of mine. She seemed to understand some of the pain I carried. I never did know why or how she could understand, but she was a great person. She listened and did not judge me. She saw that I was smiling a bit and I told her about meeting Bobby earlier.

As we talked, I opened my locker. There inside was a folded piece of paper. Carol did not seem to be surprised as I opened it, and she told me that she knew all about Bobby. She gave him my locker number and he had put the note inside.

The note was simple and short, but it must have been the most beautiful thing I had ever read. It offered me some hope and made my heart flutter. He would never know how much that little note went toward healing a hurting heart at that moment. Suddenly I couldn't wait until the end of the day so I could meet him at my locker as he had asked. I must have floated through the day.

After classes I quickly walked toward my locker. My heart was beating fast, some in anticipation and some in fear. Could this be a cruel joke? Will he really come?

I know my smile must have rivaled any ray of sunshine as I approached my locker and saw him standing there with a smile, waiting for me.

He and I talked and talked and promised to meet again in the morning. He briefly touched his lips to mine, and I felt like a princess. I didn't care what was waiting to insult me now! I was somebody that somebody else wanted to get to know! Look out world, I am not giving up now!

Slowly I learned that someone did not need to walk through life with her eyes downward. There was a whole new world out there to explore. I knew that my parents would never understand, so there was no way I would ever share my new and special secret. I would be especially careful to guard this precious friendship so I could cherish it.

Special moments were shared as I learned that Bobby too knew the pain of being alone. His mother had left his life early on, and he was put into foster care for many years. He understood and helped to share some of the pain and to understand that life isn't always bad. Together we faced each new day head on, leaning on each other and knowing that together, alone was nice!

A stolen kiss or an embrace was more healing than any medicine man could invent.

As special as those days were, they too did not last. My heart was broken when Bob told me that his birth mother had requested that he and his siblings be returned to her care. It meant that he would have to move away. My life had looked so much better, but alas, the clouds were just gathering.

Sleep was hard to come by for many days after he left. I would often cry myself to sleep. I met an old friend who had not visited me for quite a long time. My dreams again haunted me as I watched the back of my mother's head walk away from me and out of my life, but now I faced an added part to that dream. I was helplessly watching as that person turned around, and it was my beloved Bobby walking away from me.

As I tried to avoid it, I slipped back into the same feelings of being alone in the world. I did not care anymore who said what. My young heart had great difficulties dealing with the wounds and loneliness. Young love is so beautiful, but it is also painful when it leaves one standing helpless and alone. What had I done that I would have to feel such pain and abandonment yet again?

I lived through the pain of losing my first love. I was sure that for anyone it was a joyful memory but painful when it faded away. I was older then and had had a lifetime to learn how to block out some of the pain and disappointment. I was not to know at that time, but shortly after Bobby moved away, I would meet the wonderful man who would be even better medicine and touch my life in a much more precious way. He was the man who would become my soul mate, my husband, and father to my wonderful children. I was too young to know it, but God often opens another door with more wonderful things in life when one is closed.

Young Love/ Stolen Love

Young love is like a rose, just waiting to bloom.

It brings a quiet beauty to everything in its room.

It makes the music sweeter, the clouds fluffy white

And everything glitters like diamonds in the night,

Love is like a promise, a beginning to see

All the wonderful mysteries that life can be.

It leaves you floating through each new day

And with that special someone you always find your way.

But love can be like a sharp pain, deep and hard to bear

Leaving you wondering if anyone does care.

It makes life a bit more bitter, like a thief that stole your light.

Love is like an enemy that leaves you to cry at night.

Love is like a ghost, disappearing but yet still there

With millions of little tears for you bear.

Love is like a balloon floating out of sight

Taking all the beauty of life and spilling it into the night.

I loved you and I lost you, now what do I do?

My heart is deeply wounded and breaking in two.

For I loved you like no other that came into my life

Now my mind, spirit and body are filled with a painful strife.

All Grown Up

Finally, graduation is over, and I was on my road to becoming an adult. I had overcome so much of my pain, and I found that Jesus Christ forgives all sins and can make our lives so much better if we let him. I had heard the same story many times in my life, but I was not ready to listen or to let the pain and sadness that I had carried for so long be totally washed away by him.

I am so thankful that God had given me Frank. He is a wonderful man, gentle and caring. He is a good looking man that who does wonders for me. I enjoy our time together. I know that he is a gift from God, and he is the one I hope to spend my life with.

I got a job working at a state institution working with mentally challenged folks and moved into my own apartment, I love my work, however challenging and even dangerous it can sometimes be. I can finally show love and help to someone who needs it. I wanted to work in an orphanage so I could help children face what I had faced and hopefully not carry too many scars. However, there were no orphanages in our area anymore. So instead, I took the civil service test to work with the handicapped individuals and was employed by the state.

The first night I worked at the institution I was very nervous; Can I handle this job?

The nurse told me that they were scheduling me to work the "older gentlemen's ward". A challenge indeed. If someone could last for a week for two there, they would probably be able to handle the job anywhere, I was told.

The first night wasn't so bad as I had feared but I sure was embarrassed. I had lived a sheltered life, in many ways, and I was not ready for seeing a grown man naked and needing care. It was something of a shock to me when another worker told me I had to give a man a urinal. I stared at him and asked, "How do I do that?"

He just laughed as he told me how. When I stated that I needed two washcloths, he laughed again. I used one to touch the man and one to hold the urinal. (We did not use gloves back then). I did the task but was really embarrassed. Later, the staff person laughed and told me, "You do know that all you would have had to do is ask the man to help you. He would have done it himself. I just wanted to see how you would handle it." It seemed like a joke to that staff person that I was as green as a new cabbage.

The next morning was really a challenge. Upon getting everyone up and out of bed and ready for the day, I encountered a problem that brought fear to my heart and tears to my eyes. Two gentlemen in wheelchairs backed me into a corner of the cubicle. I was petrified as they laughed and kept pushing me backwards. I finally broke down and cried out for help.

When I finally calmed down and someone "helped me" by encouraging the two men to leave me alone, I wondered if I was cut out for the job. The young man that was training me had finished laughing at me and finally told me that the two men who had cornered me were just joking. One was a paraplegic who could only move his fingers to operate his electric wheelchair and the other one was just trying to tease me. I knew then that I could either let it defeat me or accept it as a prank and act like a real employee who can handle anything. I chose to stand up and be firm. Later, both of the men became very close to me and made my job both interesting and rewarding.

There were times when my resolve to care for people wavered. I wanted to do my best and brighten someone's day, but many times it was more important to provide just the basic necessities of care, as the staffing ratios were low. I was later moved to work between several other wards. I began working with babies, older women, younger women, and again the older gentleman. Many of the clients living at this institution touched my life. I yearned to be able to spend more time showing them how special they are but the last time constraints kept us so busy each and every day more.

I loved my job and it indeed touched my life I tried to impact the lives of my clients or charges but I must honestly say that the job impacted my life in a deep and meaningful way. It made me thankful for the help and blessings that God is giving me. It made me pray for healthy children and it made me feel worthwhile. I don't think a lot of healing came until I took care of those people who had so little but their million dollar smiles were worth more than worldly riches. A hug was something that was so rewarding and made me feel more comfortable in the job I was doing.

While working the night shift one night I was preparing medications to give to the clients I never liked the smile of penicillin and was very allergic to it. Just the smell of the medication sent my head spinning and made my stomach weak. I tried to fight the feeling but passed out briefly. I wasn't sick but something wasn't right. I soon learned that my life was going to change again, drastically but this time what joy the changes would bring.

What A Wonderful Surprise

The morning seemed to come too soon, and I was always tired I couldn't eat anything and was so weak all the time. I thought the flu, or something was going around. Subconsciously I knew the real reason for all the problems but silly me thought only other girls got caught

I made an appointment with a doctor in the town I was living in. He asked many questions on my first visit. After my exam he came back in and asked me if I was ready to be a parent. He said he could congratulate me, or other procedures could be done. After I recovered from the shock and the insult of his statement, I told him that I was more than ready I was overjoyed. I couldn't stop smiling as I left his office.

It might have taken all of an hour or two for me to face the reality. *I am only 18 and I'm single. I know that Frank is a wonderful man, but how will he feel? Will I be a good mother? Can I show a child love when it has been in such short demand in my life? Can I handle it all financially?* So many questions ran through my mind. I knew that it would be a challenge, but I also knew that no one or nothing would take that precious little blessing from me.

As the time came for Frank to visit that evening, I became a little scared. *How would I tell him and what would he say?* I was thinking back to the Valentine's Day we had celebrated together. I had jokingly got him a card that said, Happy Valentine's Day- I am pregnant. Inside it said just joking. I realized that the joke was on me because I was already expecting his baby. I sure hoped he would not be upset.

I knew that Frank was a great young man, but I did not know just how great until that evening. When we had our talk, I said that I did not expect anything of him; that I could raise the child. I also told him what the doctor had suggested about other procedures. I said that I would never consider harming the child. He took me in his arms and thanked me. He actually thanked me for not even considering that. He told me that the baby was his and he wanted to get married and become a daddy. He went out to his car and brought one of his tapes and played it for me. The song he played was called, Having my Baby. it's sang, "what a wonderful way of saying that you love me. That precious memory will stay in my mind forever.

Together we would face this challenge. But expecting the prospect of parenthood together, we would have the thing I want at most in my life- someone of my own to love and cherish. Frank taught me what love is, but little did I know that even that deep love did not compare to the love a mother feels for her child, even when it's unborn.

After our wedding not every day was filled with wonderful times. We had our share of troubles, as young couples do, but we had love and the joy we shared as we waited for the birth of our first child.

As I gazed down at the little baby being born, I was overwhelmed with joy. Birth is such a precious miracle. I was speechless from such an overpowering sense of awe and thankfulness. A beautiful little boy was laid on my stomach. My eyes were full of tears as I counted 10 little fingers and 10 little toes. His little face looked like the face of an Angel. All the labor had been hard, but I felt renewed with hope. As I looked into his father's face, I realized that he too was speechless. He tenderly gave me a kiss and his eyes held that trace of tears also.

Such pride and joy are hard to contain. I knew that I was happy for our child, but I never realized that someone could love a tiny being so much. As I gazed at his little face and held him to me, I knew at that moment that I would gladly die to protect that precious little being.

We chose his name Eric Guy Troup, using my dad's name for his middle name. Perhaps my dad would know that no matter how I acted as I was growing up, I was thankful that my parents did not turn their back on me; even with all the problems I gave them growing up.

I could barely wait until I could take my precious little boy home and Frank and I could become parents. Frank was so proud, and we talked so much about all the things we wanted to do with our little boy. Soon we would be going home, and our new life would begin. The day before we were to be discharged my doctor came into my room. He seemed quite concerned. I knew

I was feeling good and had recovered from the anemia that I had during the pregnancy. "Your baby has yellow jaundice," he explained to me. "His bilirubin count was very high. The procedure for this is to put him under a special light. A nurse will put a little mask over the baby's eyes, and a diaper on him, and, put him under this special light. The problem is that the baby has to stay at the hospital for this procedure."

My heart was broken as I rode home from the hospital that day. I felt like I was leaving behind my promise for the future, my very reason for living. I counted the days until I could bring him home. On the day that I was expecting to bring him home, I did receive a call from the doctor.

During the night Eric had started to vomit and had lost a lot of weight. They were so concerned that they wanted him transferred to the Geisinger Hospital emergency room, which specializes in infant emergencies. It was a long drive to the hospital that day. We were to follow the nurse who would make the drive from one hospital to the other hospital. When we arrived at the hospital the nurse said that I could ride along with her to the Geisinger, and I could hold Eric in my arms. Frank followed behind in our car. I am sure his heart must have been breaking as much as mine, but at least I was holding the baby. How much he must have suffered but his strength is what carried me through this all. The ride to the Geisinger hospital was much too short. It was pure agony as I handed Eric over to the nurses and doctors in the intensive care unit. He looked so much healthier than the other babies there and he was so much bigger. It was with a broken heart that I once again left my baby in the care of the nurses and doctors and headed home with his daddy. I admired Frank for the way he handled all my tears and insecurities. I would have liked to stay with the baby at the hospital the whole time, but I was still recuperating and there was no way that I could stay nearby. The trips to and from the hospital were exhausting, but I treasured the times I could sit in the rocker and hold baby Eric and feed him a bottle.

His little feet were like pincushions from all the blood work the doctors did. He had to swallow barium and have his digestive system X rayed. The doctors took spinal fluid and tested it. How many tests can they do in one little baby?

Eric had been moved from intensive care to a regular room two days before I was to go up for the next visit.

He seemed to be doing quite well as we were basically waiting for all the test results.

As the doctor approached the room, I was a bit nervous. *Is it good news or bad news that he is bringing?*

When he got closer, I saw he was smiling. Surely this meant that he had good news. Sure enough, his first words were "How would you like to take that little guy home?"

He explained that the test results were back and all they could find was that we had a healthy baby that had a weak digestive system. If I was able to feed him every two hours, the doctors would let me take him home.

Frank and I were overjoyed as we carried our baby son out to the car and prepared for our journey home. "Thank *you, God, for watching over our little boy and giving us such a miracle."* I prayed.

I could not take my eyes off his little face, and I held him even when he was sleeping. He was such a precious little boy and as he grew, we were amazed to see how just wonderful a child he really was.

Our Little Bundle Of Spice

Oh, how wonderful it is being a mother. I wonder if I will be able to love this new baby as much as my precious Eric.

I had just come back from seeing my doctor and although initially I was told that I had a gallstone, my persistence paid off. Today the doctor told me that I would deliver this little gallstone in about 7 months. Frank and I were both excited, but to be truthful, I was a little afraid.

I knew that God had given me a wonderful gift when he gave me a son to love. I knew that I had strong enough maternal love for him, but I wondered if a mother's love could just extend itself to others as deeply as it does for the first child. I prayed to God that he would help me and bless us both with a healthy happy baby. I secretly hoped we would have a baby girl.

As the days grew into months, and the time neared to have the baby, I was certain that God was going to give me a little girl. I didn't know how I knew it; I was just so certain that I was going to have my little Christina. I have always loved that name and hopefully I would be able to use it as part of my family.

After a long time in labor, I was so happy to hear the words that I longed to hear. "Congratulations Mr. and Mrs. Troup, you have a little girl." When I looked into that tiny little face of delicate features, and saw perfect little fingers grasp onto mine, I knew the answer to my fears. I was filled with the most wonderful feeling of awe and love. I knew I could love as many children as the good Lord blessed me with. This tiny little girl was a blessing and every bit as precious as her big brother. I was filled with plans to form a relationship with my daughter that I had never had in my life. The future looked so wonderful, and I was so happy that words could never explain it.

My little girl would indeed change my life. She would show me so much unconditional love and would help me to heal many more wounds. She would also give me a hunger- a hunger to find the parents and precious brothers that fate had taken from me. I longed to be able to share the wonderful life that God had given me with my birth brothers and my dad. My memories of him were sweet and sometimes I longed to be able to answer the questions that were still often a source of pain. I must say that the memories I carried of my mother were quite bitter ones that I did not like to bring up often. I longed for my children to know their heritage and to share all the happiness that I felt those days. God is surely a good God and I had so many blessings to share.

The tiny bundle of sweetness would grow to be a wonderful young lady who would become my best friend. I cherished the close Mother-Daughter bond we shared. What a true blessing a daughter is.

Christina

A sweet little bundle that God has given us today
A gentle sweet daughter to show the way.
Christina Arlene what a beautiful song to me
For you are a Princess, a vast beauty I see.

A heart that was hurting was healed with love,
And was given such a special blessing from above.
When I look into your tiny face
My heart is full of love and grace!

Your daddy is just as proud as can be
for he is just as thankful as me.
I know your hand will hold his heart
For daddy's little girl has a special part.

I can't wait to introduce you to your Big Brother,
For he is a sweetie like no other!
He will love you and hold your hand
And together as a family we will stand.

You are the answer to a prayer for me;
An example of love in great beauty.
May God guide me as I help you to grow
For I treasure you more than you will ever know!

Finding My Brother

With the birth of my two children, I longed to find my brothers even more than ever. I had been trying for years to find them. I remembered our family name, their nicknames, and the general area of where my two older brothers had been adopted. I scoured over every available telephone book in the area looking for someone named David Hoover.

A few months ago, I found a name in the book that reflected an address in the general vicinity of where they should have grown up. I remembered my big brother David and my older brother (only by Goliath). I remember that we used to call them that because they would fight a lot. I was pretty sure that no one with that name would be listed and how I excited I was when I did find a listing for David Hoover. I wasted no time in calling the number and explained how I was adopted and was looking for my brother.

Imagine my disappointment when he told me he was from a large family and knew all of his family history. He was a very nice man and explained that he would be happy to ask relatives and relay any information to me. For this reason I did not get excited when I was told that I had a call from David.

"You don't understand my husband said, this is not the gentleman that you have been speaking to. This man said he is looking for his little sister." I guess I was a bit leery at the time as I had found so many disappointments along my search. I cautiously called the number given and waited when the phone was answered. I felt hot, cold, nervous and even a bit scared. What if this was the one that I have been hoping for so long?

The voice that came on the line was young and friendly. We had only spoken a few words when he asked the $1,000,000 question "Are you by any chance looking for two brothers you have not seen for almost 16 years?" With tears in my voice I replied that I had been looking for so long and had almost given up hope. For the next hour or so, we spoke as cautious strangers who longed to have many questions answered. We agreed that we had waited long enough and we set up a meeting for the next day.

Is my search truly over? Is he really my Big Brother?

He said he grew up with our oldest brother and his name wasn't Goliath but Robert. Memories flashed through my mind of being so young and having two Big Brothers to spoil me as we ran through the carnival grounds where my parents were working. I remembered songs being sung, dancers in their bright colors, cotton candy, and my pigtails being pulled. The tears fell like drops of rain but would stop long enough for me to laugh away some of the pain. Disappointment had been riding on the emotional train for all the years we had missed knowing each other.

Do my brothers like to play in the rain? Do they enjoy long walks in the woods? Have they craved to know the little sister who was once a part of their Life? What do they think about when they look back into the recesses of their memories? Is there pain, confusion, a craving for someone to call their own? Do they feel as

I did many nights that life is not always so fair or did they carry a hope and a belief that one day we would once again be reunited and find some family ties?

It would seem that perhaps tomorrow some of my questions might be answered. As I met this stranger who was perhaps my long-lost Big Brother.

The night was long and little sleep was gained as I looked forward to the following day. How was I going to get through a whole day of work before I knew the answers I craved to find? The day loomed long and the emotions that I carried with me throughout the day almost overwhelmed me. The hours seemed to fly on by then in the same instance drag on forever. I would stop and catch my breath from the sheer wonder of expectations and in the next moment fear and uncertainty would be my companion.

What if this person is not who I am expecting? What if he is someone else's Big Brother? Will I face a stranger or will I know him on sight? So many questions, so many expectations and so many emotions it was draining.

Finally, the day grew to a close and as I waited for the clock to strike three so I could go to the appointed meeting place. I was restless and nervous my boss finally said to me, "go ahead you have waited long enough see if this is what you have been searching for so long."

I had only to drive a short 3 miles to the car dealership where we agreed to meet. My hands were shaking and my mouth was dry. As I turned into the lot, waiting there was a small car with a young gentleman sitting in it. I took a deep breath and prepared to leave my car and walk over. But coming toward me was a stranger who was so familiar and so much like the face I saw in the mirror each morning. It was almost like an older version of the younger brother I was lucky enough to grow up with. It was no stranger coming toward me. There was no mistake, my heart stopped beating for a brief moment before it kicked into over-drive. He was the person I had been searching for, one of the brothers I held dear in my heart and my memories for 16 long years. No words were spoken as he looked into my face and I into his. We merely acknowledged each other with tears in our eyes and gave each other a long awaited hug. Tears fell and we both felt the kinship and knowledge that we had found our way home to our family ties once more.

There were horns blowing as my friends drove by on their way home from work. It seemed like many of them had the curiosity and wondered if my story was a story come true that one only hears about but seldom witnesses. The horns were like a congratulation and it made both my brother and me smile.

The day would not go down in history and no one may ever remember the date; however February 11th, 1978, will forever be a historical and magical day to me. It was the day that one of my dreams came true and many questions were answered. The path toward healing had begun.

I told David that his niece would turn one year old the following day February 12th. He quickly decided that he would like to become a part of our family immediately. My beautiful daughter can proudly say that she had a unique and interesting 1st birthday party as it was the first day, she ever met her uncle David. We laughed, we cried, and we grew to know each other and appreciate the blessing of finding each other.

I was so thankful for finding David and getting to know my brother. It had been 16 years since I had seen my brothers and David also told me that he'd had the phone number for Bobby, our older brother.

It Has Been A Long Time ...

It's been a long time, many days gone by,
And still, we ponder the question, "Why?"
Why did I happen, this pain of the past?
That makes one think the agony will forever last?

It is a terrible feeling to be all alone,
It mars your mind and turns the heart to stone.
This silence it carries is louder than a gun
And from the scars you can never run.

It is torture to know someone didn't care
So, in the middle of silence, you are sitting there.
Thinking one human had so little compassion to give
It stained and darkened the lives we all had to live.

I carry a hate so deep within my heart,
A longing, a want, a need never to part.
A desire to find in the mysterious past

The family closedness I wished forever to last.

Now as an adult with a new feeling of hope
I cling to my desire like a life-saving rope.
Perhaps someday my doors will open wide
And I will see my whole family gathered inside.

"Oh God," I pray late at night
Keep us all within your sight.
Thank you for the blessing of my brother so dear
For today you brought him right here!"

For my brother, I thank you Dear Lord.

California Adventure

I called Bobby and spoke to him in California. As soon as we started talking the years had just melted away and we were brother and sister once more. We laughed, we cried, and we compared memories. It was uncanny how many things I remembered that matched his memories. Perhaps three years old is old enough to remember such things correctly when they impact you so much.

Bobby remembered going for ice cream and coming home to see our mother driving away in a big car. I told him how I remembered watching the car take her away forever. I told him I could remember the house. It was situated near a railroad track, and he told me that he remembered that one ran near our backyard.

We reminisced and planned on getting to know each other better.

Peggy, Bobby's wife, was such a wonderful person. I had a sister-in-law with whom I could talk to and become friends. They had a little baby, and I was excited about being an aunt to Jason. We shared pictures and marveled how much our children resembled each other. It seemed like we were not strangers who were just finding each other, but, rather like a sister and brother who just had a minor hurdle to overcome to become close and reunited as a family.

We wrote often and spoke with each other on the phone. Many of our letters reflected much of the same hurt, pain, and delusion growing up. Bobby had a lot of trouble coping with the adoption as I had growing up. We both seemed to find that anger was a constant companion when we were adolescents. Finally, someone could understand what I had felt and the pain and not judge me for some of the hate I carried.

As the weeks turn into months, we continued to get to know each other. Plans were made for my family and me to travel to California and spend a week with my brother and his family.

The flight to California was an experience, as excitement was a constant companion. Traveling with two small children was always a challenge but even more so as I was expecting another little one.

Many thoughts flowed through my mind during the flight, but the children kept me busy and made the waiting seem insignificant.

Upon arriving at the airport, I found that I did not need to look far to find my brother. There waiting for us was another answer to many of my prayers. I looked into the eyes of my big brother for the first time. I felt again like I was coming home after a long vacation. I felt like this was meant to be, and as he, Peggy, and their beautiful little baby boy approached, tears welled up in my eyes and flowed down my cheeks as raindrops of happiness.

The tears washed away many painful memories and helped to heal some of the scars that had been carried way too long.

I knew that a new relationship could have trials and problems, but he was my big brother, the one who used to pull my pigtails, but would stand up to any other bully that would dare try to hurt his baby sister.

We spend a week getting to know each other. We would often talk till late into the night. We did not plan a lot of busy things to do during the week. We wanted to enjoy getting to know each other and becoming friends as well as siblings. I fell in love with a baby boy with bewitching blue eyes, and they fell in love with two little impish creatures with matching blue eyes.

Highlights of the week were going to an amusement park and sightseeing in San Francisco, but the most enjoyable and memorable time would be when we just went to a local park for a picnic and played and joked around a lot.

The blessings in my life were multiplying, and I was so thankful for finding Bobby and his wife. His little boy was a precious addition. It felt like I was somebody important. I had a family, and I was no longer the catsoff from someone who did not want to have a family.

Our time together flew by way too quickly. Before we left, we knew that although Bobby and I were brother and sister, we had a circle of friendship with Peggy and my wonderful Frank and all the children. That week was the beginning of a wonderful friendship that started healing for 16 years of life we had missed spending together.

Little Girl Memories

Little girl memories dance through my mind
And so many treasures within I find.
The memories of togetherness we once did share
Before our lives were burdened with care.

Together we would frolic and play,
Not knowing what would be the next day.
A family living life with great pace,
Heading for a struggling race.

A race of struggle each day anew
And drifting apart from you.
Each one to go a different road,
Separately trying to carry the load.

Many years we had only memories of one another,
Memories for me of parents and brothers,
And only a longing of what might have been before
And hope that one day we would find each other's door.

But a miracle happened on one bright day.
And so many things we both wanted to say.
For the distance of time was closed once more
And at last we all have won this war.

The war of sadness when a family parts,
That leaves many scars upon our hearts.
For a reunion took place that none could match.
A great friendship and love did hatch.

For the family I had- but never knew
Came into perspective and view.
Now, as a vacation to know you ends,
Remember, together we can now face life's bends.

So, thanks for a very special week.
With words alone, I cannot speak.
To say thank you means seems so small,
So, summing it up – we love you all!

Our Third Little Miracle

Each child is a blessing. Each child is a unique little person that has been brought into life to love and cherish. I cherished the two little children that God had blessed me with. Some days I wished I didn't have to go to work and leave them behind with a babysitter, but life can be hard sometimes, and one must do what is needed.

Frank and I agreed that if we ever had a third child, I would stay at home because childcare costs were expensive. We jokingly talked about all of that as being in the future. It was with some surprise in a great deal of nervousness that I found that I was going to have another baby. Both Eric and Christina were still in diapers, and it was a lot of work, however, the more I thought about things, the more I believed this baby was a blessing.

Earlier in our marriage, Frank and I had agreed that if we ever had more than two children I could stay home and be a full-time mommy to them. This was another dream about to come true for me.

As the time neared for the birth of the baby, I prayed again for a healthy happy baby, and I didn't care if it was a boy or a girl. Either one would be loved and cherished. The only thing that bothered me was the fact that both other pregnancies resulted in labor in excess of 20 hours. I had prayed for things to go a bit easier this time around. God is such a wonderful God, and he listened to my prayers. Shawn David came into this world before his doctor even arrived at the hospital. I was in labor for little more than an hour, and he was born before his daddy even had me registered into the hospital.

What a beautiful little boy he was. He had the biggest eyes and was born with the silkiest white hair. Sometimes I would lie there and look at him and think, *God took all my pain in my youth, doubled it up over with blessings, and taught me such great love.*

This little boy would undergo a bit of a rough time for a few months, as he remained a bit small. However, when he finally decided to start growing, he did not stop until he became a young man over 6 feet tall. Six feet tall, eyes of blue, and the biggest heart a young man could have. Almost all animals and children love him. I don't doubt why, though, for his smile and his laughter reaches right up to include his eyes, and he eludes sunshine and warmth in his own precious way.

Life's Little Blessings

Three children who were growing and blessing us more and more each day made our lives so rich. I supplemented Frank's income by taking in some babysitting. I love children and found that I had more love in my heart that just seemed to grow and grow and more I shared it with others.

Each family of children that I took care of made an impact on our lives. It was hard to see when I encountered some that were not loved and cherished as all children should be. There was a family that I cared for that brought many issues to the surface, and my heart broke for the two tiny boys. The oldest boy was precious to his mother, but the two younger boys were just "mistakes on my way to making a daughter", the mother would say. There were days that the boys would have such sore bottoms and would be so unclean that it would break my heart. That was hard to see, and I really had to do something when the abuse started.

The boys would come less than clean and cry when it was time to go back home. Several times I saw marks on their little bodies, and it was quite clear that things weren't right. More and more the mother would stay at my house after work and talk to me. I guess she became comfortable with me because she started to hit the two younger boys in my presence. I would ask her not to do so, but she would just cry and say that she was "worn out". One day, she hit the little one, who was little more than a babe, so hard that he flew across the room. I knew that I could no longer be a part of this situation. I asked to take her children home and find another person to babysit. I could not be a part of such actions. Even though she never brought the children back and the child abuse calls were never followed up on, it was like a blister on my heart. After that I found that I was less than enthusiastic about babysitting. My heart was hurting, and I just wasn't content.

I yearned for one more baby in my life. Frank and I had both agreed that four children would be a big enough family. Although we had the other children in such quick succession, I just couldn't seem to get pregnant. With feelings of inadequacy at preventing the abuse from the other children and the yearning for another baby, I was experiencing a bit more unease, and memories were returning to haunt me. I had worked for five years in a state institution where I helped to take care of mentally challenged adults. I saw so much abuse and would often cry about how people were being treated. It was not always because of being mistreated by uncaring staff, but often times just because of circumstances. I would often think back to this time and remember the wonderful people who had touched my life and made me appreciate my healthy children and all the blessings that God had given me. When I would see a mother treat her children with less than the respect every human being deserves, I would think to back to the ones who were so challenged and wished every mother, every person, could see how precious a healthy child is. But for the grace of God, there could go any one of us, becoming physically or mentally challenged in an instant. Couldn't these parents, as well as countless other parents, see the truth?

A Very Special Girlfriend

It was during this time that my friend from high school called me. She said she was calling from Florida to chat and to see how life was treating me. We had kept in touch since school, and it was always good to hear from her. She had some news that touched me deeply. A few weeks prior, her mother had talked to her about her birth father. Her mother had finally told her the name of her father and where to find him. My friend had called her birth father and was calling from Florida because she was there visiting him. I shared with her happiness at her success. I explained that I had received a letter that revealed some information about my birth parents too. It seemed so coincidental that the news I received was from Florida too. I told her that my birth parents had gotten back together later in life and purchased a fishing camp in Florida. It seems that my birth father had died the year before, but that our mother had moved to another part of Florida. My father and she had two more children, a boy and a girl, but the person sharing the information did not know their ages. I told her the person who bought the fishing camp shared my birth mother's name and address.

I told my friend that I would not call down to Florida because their other two children could be younger, and it could be an upset to them. My friend and I spoke for a bit longer before she told me that she would talk to me again soon. Little did I know, but she had planned to call on my behalf and see how my birth mother would react. She called me back in just a few minutes. She told me that she had followed up with a call and explained to my birthmother that I was looking for my parents. She said that my birth mother had stated tearfully, "I thought they were all lost to me forever." She told my friend that she wanted to speak to me and would call me shortly.

My friend told me that she would not tie up the phone lines because "Kitty," as I remembered her as, would soon be talking to me herself.

True to her word, I did receive a call from my birth mother. She cried, I cried, and we both spoke for a long time. She asked me about things and said she wanted so much to meet me. We had a lot to talk about. The feelings of resentment and hate that had carried on my life were gone. I really wanted to give this a chance.

I could hardly wait to call my Big Brother, Bob, and tell him about the conversation. Perhaps I would be able to have a relationship with her and find the mother I had always longed to have in my life.

She seemed interested in learning about her adult children and grandchildren. Bob was as excited as I was and called her immediately. It wasn't more than a day later that he called me and asked me to go down to Florida with him to see our "Mother".

An Emotional Trip

I knew that our trip was going to be an emotional trip. I was so sure everything would be alright. After all, I was with my Big Brother Bobby. I had put him on a pedestal and knew that he could always make things right. I sometimes felt like the years we were separated from each other had not happened. I felt like he was my Big Brother, and he would be able to make it all workout for us. So many questions were running through my mind, but I put out all thoughts of anything negative and concentrating on meeting my new / old family for the first time. I would see my mother for the first time in 21 years. As the last few miles approached, my mind was spinning, and my stomach was filled with butterflies. I wanted to see the woman who had given birth to me, and maybe she could tell me something that would make everything alright. Maybe there were good reasons why she walked away from us. At least now some questions might be answered and maybe, just maybe, some scars could be healed. How I hoped they could. She sounded so anxious to see us, and she told me that she wanted to get to know the baby girl who was torn from her life.

With many tears and hugs, I greeted my mother, sister and brother. How sweet and handsome my little brother was. He and I immediately formed a bond, and we shared many quiet moments, going for walks, and talking about our lives. Our mother had many questions for us, but we shied away from any real issues for the first few days. Finally, one day I asked her what really happened when we were left all alone. She did not know what memories I carried, and I did not want to tell her at this time. I wanted to give her a chance to tell her side of the sad story that shattered a young life and heart. "I worked evenings at a bar, our mother stated. One night when I came home, your father was very angry and started to hit me. He hurt me quite badly, and I sent you children out with a babysitter for ice cream. When you came home, I was just leaving for the hospital. I had broken ribs and a broken spirit and remained in the hospital for some time. When I came home, there was a note on the table from your father that simply said, "Now find your precious babies." She said she had gone to some of her family and looked and looked for us to no avail. While she was in Michigan, where our family resided, she had a nervous breakdown and was in need of help again. She stated that our father told her that if she would come home to him and prove herself, he would tell her where we were. With tears in her eyes, she said, "I guess I never proved myself because he never told me where you children got to, he made me throw away all the pictures and any mementos I had of you children." We shared many tears, and we talked about getting past all of the hurt and disillusionment that we had both shared in our lives. We wanted to have a relationship and become mother and daughter. I wanted to have a relationship with my brother and sister too. My sister was planning on getting married and was expecting a baby soon. She was very young, but our mother was going to help her, and her husband get a start in life.

One evening a visitor came to the door. He seemed so familiar, but I knew I had met him before. I didn't know why, but he seemed like someone who was a part of my life, and I thought my imagination was playing with my mind. But upon entering the house, he told me that he was my half-brother, Billy. He was our father son from one of his previous marriages. He introduced me to his daughter, and together we spoke about a life that had been touched by sadness for him too.

He told me that he was old enough when our father took us all to the orphanage. He begged him not to give his brothers and sister away to another family. He said he had volunteered to work at the carnival or whatever was needed to keep us together. He was just a young teenager at the time, but he loved his little brothers and sister. He told me stories about when we would go to the carnival shows and how I would sing and sit on his knee. He said he had many haunting dreams about a baby sister throughout his lifetime. He said one of the things that would often bother him, especially late at night, was knowing that out there somewhere he had a baby sister with no one to watch over her. He said he thought the boys were a bit tougher and could take care of themselves, but his memories of me were one of a spoiled little girl who could wrap both him and our father around her little finger. He would tell me how he and Bobby would both pull on my pigtails and tease me. He said that we were all quite close, as we had been living many months at a time in the back of a big truck. When you don't have time to make friends, he explained, your family are your best friends. One day his whole world was torn apart, and he lost four siblings that meant a lot to him. He said that many days and nights he would wander about us, but as a young adult can do, he put those thoughts behind him.

Billy admitted to growing up a bit headstrong and sometimes on the other side of the law. He said that he had to learn many lessons the hard way. He never found someone to love and cherish, as he didn't know if he really believed in all that anyway. I enjoyed our time together, and we too, said that we would keep in touch.

Our week together went by very quickly, and it was a tearful parting as we left again for Pennsylvania. Both my brother and I thought it was the start of a new life as a family. We laughed, we cried, and mostly so we grew closer as we planned for a future of healing.

I ignored little voices that contradicted anything my mother had told me. After all, she said she wanted to start over. Perhaps my memories were not as clear as I had thought. Perhaps a young child can perceive things differently than they really are. I was willing to forget all of the things that didn't seem to match up with what I remembered because this was a new start.

A new brother and a new sister, and an older half-brother and niece, and a chance to get to know my mother - what a whirlwind of emotions I carried for many weeks to follow. I was caught up in the excitement and newness of it all.

I was so preoccupied with it that I forgot all about my yearning for another child. Perhaps that was what it took, for a few weeks after I had returned from Florida and all the excitement, I began to get sick. It was a very familiar sickness and sure enough, upon my next visit to the doctor, I was told that we were going to have another precious addition to our family. My joy overwhelmed me.

Our Own Christmas Miracle

I thank God so much for all that life was bringing to me. I knew that a child was a true blessing, and I could hardly wait to make plans for our own little miracle. Christina was growing into quite a young lady at that time, and she was excited when I told her that she was going to have another baby brother or sister. Of course, she wanted a baby sister. Shawn who was almost 5, didn't seem too excited about the whole affair, but Eric was very excited too.

Christina was my little shadow, so it seems so natural to include her in the birth plans. We went to the library and got books about pregnancy, and when I went to hear the baby's heartbeat for the first time, she went along to the doctor's office. My doctor was amazed at the questions a little girl of seven would ask. When he let us hear the heartbeat, Christina had her little tape recorder and made a tape of it. She was so proud and showed maturity and excitement well beyond her years. She was sure that she was going to have a baby sister, and the doctor told her that she probably would. We spent the following months thinking of the baby as a little girl. The doctor told Christina that she would probably have a baby sister by Christmas.

Christmas Eve came, and I asked if we could unwrap the children's presents. Frank said, "This is unusual, why not wait for Christmas morning?" I told him that the next morning I would be in the hospital. I was so certain that the baby was going to be born for Christmas, even though the doctor had told me that I probably would now have the baby around New Years. I don't know why I knew; I just knew that in my heart I wanted to have a special time with my husband and three precious babies now. As Christina unwrapped her big gift, she was all smiles to receive a welcome home baby doll. The doll looked like a real baby. As she showed it to me, I said "soon I will have the baby like this, only it will be a real one." She and her brothers laughed and continued to unwrap their gift with squeals of laughter. What a precious time it was. Children make every day more special, and the holidays were made especially wonderful because of them. As everyone finished unwrapping gifts, I started to crawl on the floor to clean up the mess. My back bothered me a little bit, but not too much. As I stood, my water broke, and I knew that I was going to give birth that night. The weather was bitter outside, so I asked Frank to call the ambulance and take the children to his mothers. I said, my water broke, and Shawn ran to the kitchen, pushed a chair to the sink, and said, "No, mommy it is working here." Frank and I shared a laugh over his innocent remark as we hurriedly got the children ready to go to their grandparents. They lived next door on the farm, so it was just a short distance to take them, which was good because the snow was rather thick outside, and it was very cold.

The ambulance was supposed to transport me to the hospital. When Frank returned from his parents, I told him I hoped they would hurry. I feared that the baby was ready to be born there and then. I don't think he believed me, but I know he was a bit nervous as the ambulance finally arrived 20 minutes later. As the two young men and one lady came into the house, they wanted to interview me. I explained that there was no time, for this was my fourth child, and I had an extremely quick delivery the last time. I felt the child was due to be born. Each person looked at each other, and I was soon informed that not one of them had ever delivered a baby before. As they helped me onto the stretcher, the lady said that she knew it was time. I was afraid, as she told me that the baby was breech. I prayed and asked God to help us through the birth. He heard my prayer; During one of the contractions, the baby slipped back inside and was born tiny feet first period no one had turned our little bundle, and we all agreed that his was a special birth and that he had a guardian Angel at his birth. I told the lady who handled his birth that perhaps she was the Angel. She said that she had done what she had been trained to do. As the baby emerged, it was such a welcome sound to hear his little cries. As much as we had been planning on our little girl, I asked, "Are you sure when she said it was a baby boy. What a silly question! But with the good-natured mood that she had shown us all night, she said, "I was nervous and did not know exactly what to do, but this is one thing I do know about it I know he is a boy. Do you want to send him back? Maybe wait for a little girl?" How we laughed when I looked into that precious little face, all I saw was a mirror image of his Big Brother. How thankful and wonderful our miracle was. I have never had any more precious Christmas gift nor felt

God's love so keenly as on that holiday. A precious little baby boy, born on Christmas Eve, the very night of God's own son's birth, was another blessing, another miracle, and a promise of life and love.

The little boy would grow to be a tall young man that I reminded often, "God has a plan for you, young man. He had a hand in your creation, your birth, and your life. Let him lead you into a life of greatness."

A New Day, A New Blessing

Each new day is a bright new adventure. Each day brings new questions, new trials, and sometimes tears, sometimes happiness. We should always treasure each new day and embrace it with anticipation of what we can learn and how we can grow. My children have grown, and life has quickly moved ahead. Some days I don't even realize how quickly time passes. I am now a grandmother and love every minute of it. I look back and realize that life has taught me patience, brought me joy, and has been a wonderful, exciting ride. I wish I could tell you that life always works out the way we want it to. I wish I could tell you that we are all one big, happy family and have overcome all of life trials and problems. But the truth is, we all make mistakes in life, and I, too, have made my share. I hope I have learned from them. I know I have truly benefited from most of my life experiences. Much pain was endured in my young life, and sometimes I let myself think about the insecurities and the weakness of it all. But mostly I think that God allowed me to endure the pain to help me prepare for the life he had already planned for me. How could a young child enduring the pain of being abandoned be turned into a blessing? How can abuse and pain become something positive? If we dwell on the life has been negative, we will never move on and appreciate all the wonderful things that it can offer. I don't look at the pain as a wound that cannot heal, but as an experience that enable me to understand and perhaps help some child or another person who may have felt some such pain. I work with mentally challenged people, and I think perhaps knowing pain can help build some compassion; I know it helps build patience. I once taught a class with a group of juvenile delinquent boys. One of the boys approached me in a very belligerent and angry way and stated that he would not participate in my class. I told him that that was his choice, but somehow, I recognized a bit of the younger me and the pain in his young face. Some boys told me that I had to make the class easy for them because they were disabled. I asked them what their disability was. When they told me they were juvenile delinquents,

I smiled and said that I understood more than they realized. I told them that juvenile delinquency is not a disability, but rather a label that society gave them or maybe what they earned. I was not there to judge or even guess. It would be their choice to wear that label and think of it as a disability, or to work hard, overcome it, and move on in their lives. I told them briefly about a little girl who did not like the world, how she had to work hard to overcome all of life's problems. The young boy who had not wanted to participate in a class must have noticed a kindred spirits because we became friends, and he was one of the best students in the class. At that moment I realized the pain that I had endured was a blessing at that point in my life.

There was a gentleman with whom I worked that was in his golden years and was afraid of human contact. He was mentally challenged as well as having some physical disabilities. He would cringe if someone would brush against him. I love to use gentle teaching and hugs and kisses in my field of work. He would watch while I would give others in his home a hug and kiss each day. It took a long time to convince him that not all human contact is dangerous. Two years after I started working with him, he actually asked me for a hug. When a few days later he placed his mouth against my cheek and gave me a kiss, I actually cried. He was such a wonderful man and taught me so much. Again, God humbled me and showed me that life lessons come at the moment when we least expect them. I have learned to be patient, to be thankful, and above all, to trust in God's unwavering love. Each day I am blessed with another new day; I want to make a joyful noise unto the Lord. I don't always feel like singing; Even some days it seems a chore to smile, but I pray for the strength to keep learning and giving, and in return I am blessed with so many gifts from God. The little girl who was abandoned, felt unloved, and lost was given so many chances in life. God led me through the pain, helped me to thrive in his sunshine, and hopefully he will lead me to accomplish more in this wonderful adventure we call life.

Crazy Mixed-Up Kid

I was born in a family where ties were not strong
And soon my parents did each other wrong.
They loved each other but for a while
But soon they both forgot how to smile.
Life was so confusing for a crazy, mixed-up kid.

So, like time on a clock their love soon passed.
Dad and kids were alone too fast.
No mother to give us love and care
No mother to take us to the fair.
Life was so lonely for a crazy mixed-up kid.

Soon Daddy's wallet got very low,
So "for our own good" we kids would have to go.
"To a better home," he said with tears,
With love to grow on for many years.
Life wasn't too easy for this crazy mixed up kid.

So, to a home with lots of love
From grown-ups and kids to little white doves.
But no real parents to love and cherish
In a place like this your spirit could perish.
Life didn't look any easier for this crazy mixed-up kid.

So, they took me to a home full of fun
Where love was there and room to run.
To people who hungered for a child they could love.
Their prayer for a child was answered from above.
Would life be any easier for this crazy mixed-up kid?

So, a man and a woman gave up their old life
To raise someone else's child, a man who had lost his wife.
If only I wouldn't have caused so much pain.
I am sorry now and so ashamed.
But life wasn't so easy for this crazy mixed-up kid.

So very much they have done for me,
But I was blind and could not see.
So, to my parents now, whatever I do
Remember I am thankful and will always love you.
Because you made life a bit easier for this crazy mixed-up kid.

Dedicated to my parents, who indeed changed their lives when they
took me into their home and made

Echoes Of Loneliness

In the darkness of a storm, there are shadows, and in the shadows, I am there.

Beyond the pigtails and shy smile, there is a little girl who has endured things beyond her precious few years. Abandoned, abused, and unloved, she yearns for a gentle touch, a warm smile, open and welcoming arms. From early childhood and through her adolescence, author Diane Troup weathered the deafening storm alone; her mother gone, her brothers ripped from her life, she was tossed from home to home, looking for someone to protect her from the savage winds of an unkind world. As she recounts her tumultuous childhood, listen to the *ECHOES OF LONELINESS ringing* through her words, see the dark clouds of